Reynolds
to the
Rescue

Reynolds to the Rescue

The Story of Hiram F. Reynolds

LIBBY HUFFMAN

Nazarene Publishing House
Kansas City, Missouri

Copyright 1985, 1990, 1995
by Nazarene Publishing House

Third Edition 1995

Printed in the
United States of America

ISBN 083-410-993X

William A. Rolfe, *Editor*
Amy R. Lofton, *Editorial Assistant*

Cover Design: Royce Ratcliff
Illustrations by: Carolyn Bowser
Photos courtesy of Nazarene Archives

Note: This book is part of the Children's Mission Study Curriculum. It is designed for use in Year V, The Mission Support Team. This study year examines the way the Church of the Nazarene resources and supports its missionaries. *Reynolds to the Rescue* has been included in the curriculum because it teaches these concepts. The people and incidents contained in this book are factual. However, the author has added conversation and details consistent with the time.

10   9   8   7   6   5   4   3   2   1

Dedicated
to the memory of
my very dear grandfather,
Rev. Franklin Leroy Spiker, Sr.,
who, on November 29, 1980,
went to live with Jesus.

Acknowledgments

To my husband, **Les,** who kept our three-and-a-half-year-old son, **Nathan,** busy so I could have quiet time to write this book.

To my dad and mom, **Noah and Lina Sullivan,** who taught me to love Jesus.

To my coworker **Lorraine Shaver,** who loaned me her brand-new typewriter for three weeks.

To **Mark York,** who gave me my first chance to write a book.

Contents

Reynolds
to the
Rescue

Life on the Farm

"Mama!" Hiram cried. "Come back! Don't leave me! Mama!"

Hiram Reynolds was six years old. His small legs were not very fast, but he ran to catch his mother. As he slowed down, he felt two strong hands lift him into the air.

"Your home is with us now, boy," Mr. Pitcher said kindly. He carried Hiram back to the farm. "You are going to live with me and my wife on our farm."

"Why did Mama leave me?" Hiram wondered as he huddled in his strange bed that night. He was frightened. Tears ran down his cheek onto his pillow.

Everything had fallen to pieces since Papa died a year ago. First his older brothers and sister had moved away to work on other people's farms so that they could earn money and go to school. Then he and Mama had to leave their home and go to live with someone else where Mama could work. Now, Mama had brought him to the Pitchers' farm. He had never seen these people before. And Mama had gone away without even saying good-bye.

13

The sad, lonely little boy sobbed quietly in the darkness. His heart felt as though it would break into pieces.

He did not know how sad his mother had been when she went away. She would never have left him if there had been any way at all for her to take care of him.

There was little time for play on the Pitcher farm. Hiram had lots of work to do. Each day, before school, he had to feed the cows, chickens, and pigs, and bring in the eggs and milk the cows. When he got home from school each day, he had to do these things again.

Hiram had only been at the Pitchers a year when Mr. Pitcher died. Then Hiram had to do all the farm work.

Mr. Pitcher left Mrs. Pitcher with many bills to pay. She could think of only one way to get more money. She would make wine! There were many fruit trees and bushes on her farm. Instead of selling fresh fruit, Mrs. Pitcher squeezed juice from the fruit and kept it in large barrels. The juice stayed in the barrels until it fermented and turned into wine.

When the wine was ready to drink, Mrs. Pitcher had parties. She sold her wine to the people who came. Men played cards, while women and children danced. Many people got drunk. Some acted funny, but others hurt people.

Hiram watched all of this. He knew it was wrong, but he soon learned to gamble and dance like everyone else at these parties.

Mrs. Pitcher began to feel guilty about her bad influence on young Hiram. She made a new rule:

"NO CARDS, NO DRINK, NO DANCE." But it was too late. Hiram was already dancing, drinking, and gambling, as well as smoking. He did not want to stop now, and Mrs. Pitcher couldn't make him.

A Letter from the Past

"Hey, Hiram, you got a letter from the big city, Chicago," the postmaster said. "Who do you know there?"

"I don't know!" Hiram answered. He picked up the envelope and looked at the name on it. "It's from my brother Allen!" he exclaimed. "I haven't seen him since I was 6—14 years ago!"

He tore open the envelope and quickly read the letter.

Dear Hiram:

Mary and I would like for you to come to Chicago and live with us. It has been so long since we last saw you.

We wish to become your good friends. There is a job here at the factory for you. The day you get into town you can start work.

Please do come.

Your brother,
Allen

"I'm sure tired of living and working on this farm," Hiram thought to himself. "It would be good to see Allen again and meet his wife, Mary. Maybe this is my chance to leave."

Hiram packed his bags and said good-bye to Mrs. Pitcher. It was hard to leave her. After all, she had been his family for 14 years. But he just had to go see his long-lost brother.

As Allen had promised, Hiram had a job and a home waiting for him. It was a Christian home. As time passed, Mary noticed Hiram's bad habits.

"Dear Father," she prayed, "help me witness to Hiram." She wanted him to be a Christian.

Days passed quickly for Hiram in his new home. Soon it was December. Everyone was getting ready for Christmas.

"Hiram, it's been a long time since you've seen your mother," Mary said. "Don't you think it would be fun to spend Christmas with her and your step-father?"

"I don't know, Mary. I haven't seen Mother for 14 years. I don't know what I would say to her. I don't even know if I would recognize her," Hiram answered.

Hiram remembered the day his mother had left him at the Pitchers' house. It still hurt to remember it. He wasn't sure he wanted to see her again.

"You'll never know until you try," Mary replied.

Hiram thought about Mary's words. "Maybe I should go." He decided to go and got ready to make the long train trip to Vermont.

Several days later, Hiram's train pulled into Landgrove station. He felt nervous. His eyes searched the group of people who met the train.

There she was! Hiram made his way to his mother. They hugged each other again and again. They both cried.

Memories flooded Hiram's mind. They were good memories of his early childhood with his mother.

The next three weeks were very happy for Hiram. He met new relatives, went sled riding, and enjoyed the Christmas holidays.

Hiram's mother was happy to have her son with her again. But, she noticed that Hiram had learned many bad habits. She was sad. She wished she could have raised Hiram.

One day Hiram told his mother he was going back to Chicago.

"Why are you crying, Mother?" Hiram asked.

"My son," she answered, "I had hoped you would stay here with me for a long time. We were apart for so many years. I would like you to stay for a while longer."

"But I don't have a job. I have to go back," Hiram reminded her.

"Hiram, I know where you can find a good-paying job," his mother said excitedly. "It is on a farm."

She told Hiram about the Stiles family. She didn't tell him that they were Christians. Hiram's mother secretly hoped that Mr. and Mrs. Stiles could help Hiram become a Christian too. She wanted him to quit drinking and smoking.

Hiram thought about what his mother said. He did like farm work, when he had some help. It was better working in the sunshine than in a dark, noisy factory. On May 1, 1875, Hiram began work on the Stiles farm.

Hiram's mother was happy. Her son was near her again, and he was living and working with a Christian family.

One Sunday morning, Mr. Stiles said, "Hiram, I'm not feeling very well today. Would you please drive my wife to church?"

"Of course," Hiram answered.

As Hiram and Mrs. Stiles rode to church, they talked.

"Are you a Christian, Hiram?" Mrs. Stiles asked.

"Ahh—well—ahh, no, ma'am, I'm not," Hiram answered nervously.

"Why not, Hiram?" she asked.

"I'm not really sure," Hiram answered slowly. "I guess because I don't think I would make a very good Christian."

"Hiram," Mrs. Stiles said, "the Lord will accept you the way you are. He will give you the strength you need to do what is right. Think about it."

Hiram did think about it—day after day, night after night. He couldn't sleep. He couldn't eat. He was miserable.

One night while he lay in bed he heard a voice say, "Hiram, I want you to give your life to Me!"

Hiram knew he wasn't dreaming. He knew God had spoken to him. But Hiram was having a difficult time giving up his bad habits. Finally, after three sleepless weeks, Hiram made a promise to God.

"Lord, if You will save me, I promise to quit smoking and drinking."

The next Sunday Hiram went to church with Mr. and Mrs. Stiles. During the service he felt that God was speaking to him about more bad habits.

Finally, Hiram prayed, "Lord, if You will save me, I will even quit gambling and dancing!" Hiram stood to his feet—while the minister was speaking—and announced: "I want God to save me. Will you pray with me?"

A gasp went through the church

"Who is this man? Why has he interrupted the service?" the people wondered. The preacher did not know God like Mrs. Stiles did. He didn't know what to do. The preacher left the church so that he could continue the service outside. The congregation followed him.

Only Mrs. Stiles and Hiram remained.

"Hiram, continue to seek God. He will save you," she encouraged. But she could not tell Hiram *how* to seek God.

As Hiram walked home, he felt discouraged. The devil tried to tempt Hiram.

"Do you really want to quit all those fun things?" the devil seemed to say.

But Hiram was determined to find God. He knelt by the side of the road and asked God to forgive his sins. Suddenly, he was filled with peace and joy! All he had needed to do was ask for forgiveness *and* believe!

In the days ahead, Hiram was tempted many times. He sometimes became discouraged. He did not know how to read the Bible for encouragement.

On the Fourth of July Hiram went with his family to the country fair. Many people were dancing. It looked like so much fun. Hiram was tempted to dance again.

"Elmer," Hiram said to his brother, "let's go home. I don't belong in a place like this."

Hiram had learned that the best way to defeat temptation is to get away from it.

A short time after this, two evangelists came to Hiram's church. They were going to have revival services. Hiram was very excited. Here was a chance to learn more about God. He attended every service. One of the evangelists asked Hiram to help. He wanted Hiram to talk to one person about God before the next service.

Hiram panicked! "I could never do that," he thought to himself. But he knew God wanted him to do it. Hiram's determination to serve his Lord won out over his fear.

The next morning he walked to the first farm he came to.

"Good morning, sir," Hiram called. His voice cracked nervously.

"Howdy, yourself," the farmer answered. "What can I do for you?"

"The Lord told me to invite you and your family to our revival service tonight," Hiram said.

"Why don't you come in and have breakfast with us?" the farmer invited.

Hiram agreed. The farmer asked Hiram to say grace. After breakfast, the family went into the living room. The farmer handed a big Bible to Hiram.

"Read something for us," he commanded.

Hiram did.

The family accepted Hiram's invitation and went to the revival. All five members of that family became Christians. A few days later, Hiram, his mother, younger brother, and that farm family were baptized. What a wonderful day that was!

Yes, Lord,
I'll Preach!

"Hiram, you must preach My Word."
"Hiram, you must preach My Word."

Hiram could not believe that God was calling him to preach.

"Lord," Hiram pleaded, "I don't have a good education. I don't know very much about the Bible. How can I preach Your Word?"

Hiram was afraid it was his own idea. "Lord, I love You. But I am not smart enough to be a preacher. Why, I just learned where the Book of Genesis is."

Every day and every night Hiram was troubled about this call to preach. Was it really from God?

One clear, bright night, Hiram was lying on his bed. He had tossed and turned for hours. He looked through a window and saw the stars. It seemed as though they, too, were saying, **"You must preach! You must preach!"**

Hiram jumped out of bed. "Lord, please help me know if this is really Your will."

Hiram decided to look for the answer in his Bible. He prayed, "Lord, if You are really calling me to preach, show me in Your Word."

Hiram opened his Bible. The first words he saw were **"Preach the gospel."** Hiram was still not convinced. "That could have been a coincidence," he thought. Once again Hiram prayed. "Lord, I will use my brand-new Bible. The pages have not been used too much. They will open to any page. If You really want me to preach, show me." Again Hiram opened his Bible—his brand-new Bible!—and the first words he saw were **"Preach the gospel."** Hiram's Bible fell from his hands onto the floor. As Hiram knelt on the floor beside his Bible, he again read these words, **"Preach the gospel!"**

"Lord, I love You. You know that I want to serve You. Now I am sure You want me to be a preacher. With Your help, I will be," Hiram promised.

Suddenly, he thought about Stella, beautiful Stella. She was the only girl Hiram had ever loved.

"Lord, I can't be a preacher. Preachers are poor. How can I ask Stella to marry me when I won't make enough money to support her?" He felt sure he would lose Stella forever.

Hiram decided to work out his problem by himself. "I know what I will do," he thought. "I won't tell anyone about my call. I won't become a preacher. I'll find a different job."

Hiram started to work for Stella's father in his lumberyard. One cold morning the lumber camp woke up to four inches of new snow.

"Hiram," his boss said, "I need you to drive the bobsled down the mountainside to pick up a shipment of wood."

Hiram did not want to go. He knew it would be dangerous driving in the snow. But he did what his boss asked him to do.

As he sped along in the bobsled, suddenly Hiram hit a deep hole. The front of the bobsled dipped down. Hiram was thrown partway out of the sled. His feet were caught and his head hung down close to the ground. Hiram was trapped! To make things worse, the horses started to run again! Hiram knew he didn't have long to live. He was completely helpless.

"O God, please help me! I don't want to die," Hiram cried out.

All at once the horses stopped running. Hiram pulled himself out of the sled. Hiram knew that God had heard and answered his prayers. He prayed a humble prayer of thanks. He knew God had saved his life. "I must obey God's call," Hiram thought. "I must preach the gospel—even if it means that I can't marry Stella."

Hiram quit his job at the lumberyard. He made a very important visit to see Stella on his last day there.

"Stella," Hiram said nervously. "I love you very much. I want to marry you, but God has called me to preach. I won't be able to give you fine clothes and houses. But I want you to serve the Lord with me. You don't have to give me your answer now. I'll be back in two days to hear your answer."

Poor Hiram was so nervous he didn't give Stella a chance to talk. He walked from Stella's house that day feeling very sad. He just knew that Stella would turn him down.

Those two days c-r-a-w-l-e-d by. Hiram thought they would never end. Finally, on the special day, Hiram slowly walked to Stella's house.

"Stella," Hiram started, "you've had two days to think and pray about my proposal. Do you have an answer for me?"

"Yes," Stella began. "Hiram, I have prayed a lot about the things you said. I know that I love you too. I would be very happy to serve the Lord by your side."

Hiram couldn't believe his ears. Stella had said **yes!** He and Stella were going to get married! They decided to wait one year until Hiram finished his first year at seminary. They both knew the school for preachers would help him be a better pastor.

Hiram began seminary. He soon realized that he had a poor education. He seemed to be behind everyone else. He worked hard to catch up with his classmates. He also had to work every day at odd jobs to pay for his schooling. He was a waiter, a janitor, and a floor scrubber.

After Hiram finished his first year of seminary, he went to a meeting of church leaders from many cities. At this conference Hiram was given his first church to pastor. It was in a tiny town called Bondville, Vermont. Hiram Reynolds was now **"Rev. Reynolds."** He was finally getting a chance to preach the gospel.

It was also time for a wedding. On July 17, 1879, Hiram and Stella became Rev. and Mrs. Hiram Reynolds.

Hiram worked very hard as a pastor. He spent every morning reading the Bible, praying, and studying. In the afternoons he visited the sick and counseled people in trouble.

Hiram continued to work hard—day after day after day. One morning he started to get out of bed early as usual.

"Stella," he said, "I don't have the energy to get up. I am so tired."

Stella immediately sent for a doctor. "What could be wrong?" she wondered.

The doctor came quickly, but it took a long time to examine Hiram.

"Pastor, if you don't take better care of yourself, you will die from exhaustion," the doctor said seriously. "You must slow down. You can't keep working so hard."

"What can I do?" Hiram wondered.

"You have to do what the doctor said," Stella answered. "You must take it easy for a while."

"But the church needs a full-time pastor. I don't know what I can stop. Stella, there is so much to do."

"Then maybe you should let someone else pastor the church while you rest," Stella said. "It will only be until you are better."

Hiram didn't want to resign his church so that he could rest. He prayed and asked God what he should do.

At last he knew. Sadly, he resigned his church to rest.

A few weeks later Hiram found a job in a sawmill. But he pushed himself to work, work, work. He didn't rest like he was supposed to. Once again, he reached the point of total exhaustion.

Mr. Farmer, the man Hiram worked for, was a Christian. He noticed that something was wrong.

"Hiram," Mr. Farmer said, "would you like to go to the camp meeting services with me next week?"

"But, Mr. Farmer, I have to work to earn money for my family. I can't afford to take a week off without pay."

"Now, Hiram, hear me out. I will pay you for the week as if you had worked. I will even pay your way to the camp meeting. Now, will you go with me?"

Hiram thought this chance was too good to pass up. So he went to the camp meeting with his boss.

"You can receive the gift of the Holy Spirit," the speaker said as Hiram walked into the church. "You can have a clean heart and a pure mind. All you have to do is ask God to cleanse your heart and make you whole."

"This sounds like what I need," Hiram thought as he listened to the speaker.

After the sermon, Hiram walked to the front of the tent church. He knelt facedown in the straw. Tears ran down his face. "O God," he prayed, "cleanse my heart and mind. Make me completely Yours."

Soon Hiram felt warm from his fingertips to his toes. "Thank You, Lord," he said happily. "You have answered my prayers!"

Then Hiram asked God to heal him so that he could preach again. The Lord also answered that prayer. That night Hiram slept peacefully the whole night. How wonderful he felt the next morning! Then he had a splendid idea.

"Sir," Hiram said to the district leader, "I know God has filled me with His Holy Spirit. I know that He has also healed me physically. I am ready for a church if you have one."

"I am sorry, brother," the leader said. "All the churches are filled. No—wait! There are a couple of people who live in Plymouth, Vermont. They have no church building, no parsonage, and no money, but they want a pastor. Are you feeling up to that?"

"I'll pray about it and give you my answer today," promised Hiram.

He prayed for a very long time. At last he decided God wanted him to become the pastor at Plymouth.

"Thank You, Father," Hiram prayed. "I can be a preacher again."

Hiram worked hard. With God's help the church grew from 2 to 35 in one year.

One day a board member said, "Rev. Reynolds, we have a request. We want you to stop preaching about the Holy Spirit. We feel that you are trying to tell us how to live. We want you to stop or we will ask the leader to replace you."

Hiram was surprised. "Not preach holiness! What else could I preach about? I believe in holiness. God told me to preach holiness. I can't disobey God, even if it means I will lose this church."

Hiram went right on preaching like he always had. The board members sent a letter to the church leader. A few days later Rev. Reynolds met his leader at the train station.

"Hiram, I think you know why I am here. I agree that your church needs to hear about the Holy Spirit. But I don't think it will hurt to preach just a little less on holiness," he said. "You don't need to tell the people they shouldn't smoke or drink. Let them live the way they think they should."

"I'm glad you agree they need to hear about the Holy Spirit," Hiram said. "I think they need to know how to obey God and live right. But I'll pray about it."

Hiram did pray about it. He asked God to show him what to do. A few days later he wrote the following letter to his leader: "My Dear Elder, I respect you very much. I appreciate the kind advice you gave me the other day at the station. I have been praying like I said I would. I learned many years ago that if I disobey God, I will lose confidence in my abilities as a preacher. Though I have much respect for you, I must obey God. I will continue to preach holiness."

After preaching for 13 years, Hiram felt God calling him into a different kind of ministry. "Stella," he announced one morning, "I believe God wants me to become an evangelist."

4

A Brand-new Church

Rev. and Mrs. Reynolds moved to Montpelier, Vermont, to live when he resigned his church to become an evangelist. Hiram had to travel around to different churches. He treasured the times home with his family.

"Hiram," exclaimed Mrs. Reynolds, "our new home is beautiful. I'm glad God brought us to live in Montpelier."

"So am I, Stella," Hiram agreed. "I just hope I get to stay in town enough to enjoy it with you and the children."

Shortly after they had moved to Montpelier, Hiram heard about an association of holiness preachers. It was called the Vermont Holiness Association. It was a group of people who believed in the Holy Spirit like he did. Hiram asked to become a member. At last he had found a group that shared his beliefs. Hiram worked hard for the association.

The other members were so impressed with Rev. Reynolds that they elected him as their president. This was a real surprise for young Hiram. He worked even harder to be a good president.

Early one morning a few months later, Hiram heard a voice weakly call his name.

"Hiram! Hiram! Can you hear me? Hiram, I need you."

It was his wife. "Yes, Stella, dear. I am right here. What's the matter?" he asked anxiously.

"I don't know what's wrong with me," Stella answered. "I feel so weak and sick. I don't have any strength."

"Don't worry, dear," he soothed. "I'll pray for you. If you aren't feeling better in a little while I'll call for the doctor."

Hiram knelt and prayed for his wife. He had never seen her so sick before.

Hiram had to go to another church and hold a revival the next day. During the revival Stella got worse. Hiram sent for a doctor. He found a lady doctor. He told her about Stella and asked her to go see his sick wife.

"I am not sure I can help Mrs. Reynolds," the doctor said. "But I'll go to Montpelier tomorrow and examine her."

"Thank you so much, Doctor," Hiram said. "My wife and I appreciate it."

The next day the doctor stopped at the Reynolds home. She examined Stella carefully. Finally, she suggested that Stella see a specialist in Montpelier. Hiram was very concerned. He took his wife to see the specialist. Stella had to go back many times. After many months of treatment, Mrs. Reynolds was well and able to be with her family.

"Stella, I really don't feel right about something," Rev. Reynolds said after one of his revivals.

"What's wrong?" Stella asked.

"We both believe in holiness. I preach holiness every time I preach. I believe God wants me to. But I am very concerned about the way our church feels about holiness. I feel so sorry for the new Christians at the revivals I hold. I know some have received the Holy Spirit. But I'm worried that their preachers won't continue to preach holiness. They won't help them grow in their faith. I am frightened that many of them will turn from God and go back to living the way they did before. I'm not sure what to do about it."

"I know how you feel, Hiram; I've felt the same way," Stella said.

"I've really prayed about this. I feel God is leading us to leave our denomination," Hiram said.

"Hiram, do you realize what a big step that would be?" Stella asked. "Many people won't understand why. They'll criticize us."

"I've already thought about that, Stella," Hiram answered. "But I'm sure this is what God wants us to do. I wouldn't do it if I wasn't so sure."

"If you feel that it's right, then so do I," Stella told her husband.

So, after being members of their denomination for 20 years, Rev. and Mrs. Reynolds decided to change. It was very difficult. They had many friends in the church. But they felt it was more important to do God's will. They could not worry about what their friends would think or say.

A short time after this, Rev. and Mrs. Reynolds moved to New York. They discovered that they lived near the headquarters of the Association of Pentecostal Churches of America. It was a group of small churches that believed in holiness!

"Stella," said Hiram one evening as they ate dinner, "I believe we should join the Utica Avenue Church. It is one of the churches in the Association of Pentecostal Churches of America. It is a fine church, and they believe in holiness. What do you think?"

"I really like the people there," Stella agreed.

In 1895 Rev. and Mrs. Reynolds joined the Utica Avenue Church. At last they had found a church that believed just like they did!

The Utica Avenue Church liked Hiram and Stella too. They soon became leaders in their new church home.

In April 1897 the Association of Pentecostal Churches held their first assembly. It was a big meeting where the churches gathered to do church business. One important item of business was how the churches would send out and support their missionaries. They voted to organize a Foreign Missions Board.

"I nominate Rev. Hiram F. Reynolds to be secretary of our Foreign Missions Board," one member shouted.

"I second that nomination," another agreed.

"But I don't know anything about missions," Hiram said. "You should elect someone who knows more about our missionaries than I do."

The assembly voted. Rev. Hiram Reynolds was elected as the Foreign Missions Board's first secretary.

"I can't do this important work, Lord," Hiram prayed. "But if this is Your will for me, I will do my best for You. I will trust You to help me do it right."

Hiram felt it was important for him to learn everything he could about missions. So he began to travel. He held special meetings to raise money to send to the missionaries. He did everything he could to improve missions, pay missionaries' salaries, and build new churches.

Hiram had always been a hard worker. There was so much to be done. He worked very hard in his new job. He worked so hard that he made himself ill again. He had to be taken to a specialist.

"Mrs. Reynolds, I am afraid I have bad news for you," the doctor said quietly.

"Will my husband be all right?" Mrs. Reynolds asked anxiously.

"Your husband has had a nervous breakdown," the doctor replied. "His body is completely exhausted. He does not have the energy to do anything but rest."

"I understand, Doctor," Stella said. "I will see that he gets plenty of rest. But it won't be easy. He pushes himself so hard."

"I know. But you *must* make him rest—or else!" The doctor looked very serious.

Stella knew the doctor was right. She made a very good nurse. She watched Hiram carefully and made sure he rested.

After a few months, Hiram started to feel better. He was worried about the missionaries. Since he couldn't travel to raise money, many missionaries were having to go without things they needed.

"Stella, I have to get back on the road soon," Hiram said one day. "The missionaries need so many things. They need their salaries; they need money for their churches. I'm not much help lying here in bed."

Young Hiram and Stella Reynolds

"Oh, no, you don't, Hiram Farnham Reynolds! You will stay put until the doctor says you can leave," Stella commanded. "You have to be completely well before you start traveling again. You can't help anyone if you work yourself to death."

"You're right," Hiram agreed reluctantly. "I'm just concerned about our missionaries."

"I know, dear," Stella said. "But you need to rest right now. You can help them more by getting *completely* well so that you can get back to work."

After a few more weeks of total rest, Hiram was feeling well. He could walk around the block. He was eating better. And he was in better spirits.

"Stella," Hiram said one day, "I think I'm ready to travel again. But I have a problem."

"What's that, Hiram?" Stella asked.

"I don't have a summer suit, and I need a new pair of shoes. But we don't have any extra money to buy them with!" Hiram looked discouraged.

"The Lord knows what we need. He will provide it," Stella answered. A few days later, a large package arrived at the Reynolds home. Stella eagerly tore it open.

"Hiram! Come quickly!" she called.

"What is it?" Hiram asked.

"The Lord answered our prayers. Here's a very nice suit. You can wear it on your tour," Stella announced.

"Oh, Stella, it *is* nice," Hiram agreed. "But I still need shoes."

"Well, let's keep looking. There might be a pair of shoes in here." Stella took more things out of the box.

Sure enough, there was a brand-new pair of shoes in the bottom of the box. But they were size 10, and Hiram wore a 7½.

"Stella, what can I do? I can't wear them. They're too big!" Hiram exclaimed.

After a lot of thought and prayer, Hiram took the shoes to a shoemaker. He fitted some heavy innersoles into the toe part of each shoe. "This should work pretty well," the shoemaker said.

Hiram tried on the shoes. They fit—except they were still too big in the heels. They kept sliding off. When he walked home Hiram could hear *clump, clump, clump, clump* with every step.

Hiram went on his fund-raising tour for missions with his size 10 shoes. It was one of the most successful tours he had. He raised enough money to send some to all the missionaries. Then there was enough left over to send some new missionaries to other countries.

While Hiram was secretary of the Foreign Missions Board, he met many people. They talked a lot about church business. One important topic of conversation was about a new church that had started in California.

"Hiram," said one friend, "I have talked with the pastor of this new church, Rev. Bresee. He seems like a very fine Christian. He preaches holiness like we do. How do you feel about him?"

"Well, I've heard a lot of good things about Rev. Bresee," Hiram answered. "I think he's doing some good things. I hear that some of the churches around New York are talking about joining with Rev. Bresee's church. But I want to pray some more before I decide."

Many churches around New York were planning to join with Rev. Bresee's church. They would start a new denomination. After a lot of prayer, Hiram felt God wanted him to join too. So, in 1907, Rev. and Mrs. Reynolds joined the Church of the Nazarene.

Hiram and Stella made plans to attend the new church's first big assembly meeting. There he was elected one of the church's leaders, a general superintendent. People started calling him Dr. H. F. Reynolds.

"I think we should have an organized missionary society in the Church of the Nazarene," one pastor said.

"I agree," Dr. Bresee said.

"I nominate Dr. Hiram F. Reynolds as secretary," said another.

Once again Hiram was elected as secretary of a foreign missionary board. This time it was for the brand-new Church of the Nazarene. He worked so hard at the task that he became known as "Mr. Foreign Missionary."

Hiram Reynolds (right) with Dr. Bresee

5

Sailing, Sailing

Dr. Reynolds liked his new job. But it was very hard. There were many problems. Just a year after he was elected, another group joined the Church of the Nazarene. They had even more missionaries. How could the new church take care of all of them? There wasn't enough money to go around. Some of the people in Hiram's church didn't want the new missionaries. But they believed in holiness like Dr. Reynolds and Dr. Bresee, so they joined the new church.

It was really hard for Dr. Reynolds to help the missionaries now. There were too many of them. The missionaries wrote to churches to ask for money. Some didn't even have enough money for the things they really needed. The missionaries prayed. Hiram prayed too. Some people thought the whole missionary work would break down. But God sent Reynolds to the rescue.

"We need to set up some guidelines for supporting our missionaries," Dr. Bresee suggested. "Some are in real trouble."

"You're right," Hiram answered. "We need to remember one very important point—all the missionaries are *our* missionaries now."

"I agree, Dr. Reynolds," encouraged Dr. Bresee. "Since we have joined to form a new church, we have a lot more missionaries to care for. We need to take good care of all our missionaries. But how can we do this?"

"Some people think we have too many missionaries now," Dr. Reynolds said. "They want to bring some of them home. Others want us to leave them where they are whether we can support them or not. They say God will take care of them."

"Well, Dr. Reynolds, everyone knows we are in trouble. You are the general secretary of missions. What do you think we should do?" Dr. Bresee asked.

"A few months ago, Mr. Leslie Gay and I talked about this problem," Dr. Reynolds answered. "We came up with a plan we think will work. We need one board to supervise all the missionaries. The churches can send their missionary offerings to this board. Missionaries can write the board and tell them what they need."

"That sounds like a good idea to me," Dr. Bresee said.

Hiram had a plan to rescue the missionaries. Now he had to make the plan work. He had to make sure that the missionaries got the things they needed. It was sometimes very hard for Hiram to decide who should get the most money. He tried hard to be fair.

One day Hiram was feeling very sad.

"Tenyo Maru"

"Stella," he said. "I wish I could see for myself what our missionaries need. It is so hard to decide who should get what. I wish they were not so far away. I wish I could sit down and talk with each one."

"Maybe you can," Stella encouraged. "Why don't you talk with Dr. Bresee about this?"

"That's a good idea, Stella," Hiram said.

Hiram explained his problem.

"Hiram," said Dr. Bresee, "I think you should travel to all our mission fields. That's the best way for us to find out just what our missionaries need."

"I agree!" Hiram said. "I'll plan to leave with our next group of missionaries."

On December 1, 1913, Hiram and several new missionaries boarded the ship *Tenyo Maru*. It took them three and a half weeks to reach Japan.

Hiram Reynolds in China

Dr. Reynolds stayed with missionaries in Japan for 25 days. He helped build a Nazarene mission headquarters there. He also opened a new church. It was a busy 25 days.

From Japan, Hiram sailed to China. It was a very big country with only a few Christians. Hiram went with the first Nazarene missionaries to start the mission there.

While he was in China, Hiram heard of a holiness organization called the National Holiness Association. "Maybe they can help us get started," he thought. He arranged to meet with their leaders.

"Gentlemen," Dr. Reynolds began, "thank you for letting the Church of the Nazarene send missionaries to your beautiful country. It is good to find people who believe in holiness like we do. We want to buy some land so that we can build a church and some other buildings."

The people were very impressed with Dr. Reynolds. Their association voted to give the Church of the Nazarene a place to build a church. There were 1 million people living around it. Hiram and the missionaries were delighted.

"There are many people here who need our help," they said.

While Hiram was in China, he organized the first Chinese Church of the Nazarene. It had 13 members.

From China, Hiram traveled to India. He had sent the first missionaries to India just a few years before. They had gone as missionaries of the Association of Pentecostal Churches of America. But they all became Nazarenes when Hiram did. Now he had a chance to meet them. The missionaries were happy to see Dr. Reynolds.

After Dr. Reynolds arrived in India, one of the first places he visited was a Nazarene mission called Hallelujah Village. What a welcome he received! Everything was covered with flowers. A large sign hung from the front door. It read, **"WELCOME, DR. REYNOLDS."** About 120 people sang hymns and paraded around Dr. Reynolds. Hiram felt very welcomed.

Dr. Reynolds kept very busy while he was in India. Some of the missionaries at Hallelujah Village were returning to the United States. Dr. Reynolds had to find a new mission superintendent. He asked Rev. and Mrs. Leighton S. Tracy to come see him. Rev. Tracy was in charge of Nazarene missions in western India, more than a thousand miles from Hallelujah Village.

As the two men visited one afternoon, Dr. Reynolds said, "Rev. Tracy, I have a special favor to ask. We must have a superintendent for our work here in eastern India. Do you think you could add that job to what you are already doing?"

Gate of Hallelujah Village

Rev. Tracy looked thoughtful. "I'll have to pray about it before I can give you an answer," he said.

Later, Rev. Tracy agreed to become superintendent of all the missions in both east and west India. After the other missionaries went home, Hallelujah Village was desperate for help. Dr. Reynolds canceled all his appointments and stayed at the mission until the Tracys could move to their new home.

After Rev. and Mrs. Tracy were settled at Hallelujah Village, Dr. Reynolds headed for Africa.

Africa was 6,000 miles from India. It took 27 days to get there. When Hiram finally arrived, Harmon Schmelzenbach met him at the ship.

"Dr. Reynolds, it's a long, rough ride to the mission," Harmon warned.

Hiram didn't know what Rev. Schmelzenbach meant, but he soon found out. After a 100-mile train ride, they bought supplies and loaded them into a wagon. It took several days. At night Hiram slept in the wagon and Harmon slept on the ground under it. The next morning Hiram rode on a mule. Harmon thought they could travel faster that way. When he wrote to Stella after that, Hiram had many new experiences to tell her.

While Dr. Reynolds was in Swaziland, he held baptismal services, dedicated a new stone church, and held daily conferences with the missionaries.

"Dr. Reynolds, I really appreciate the time you give us each day," Harmon said. "It makes us feel like you really care about us. Sometimes we feel that everyone forgets us. But your visit has made us feel there are people who care and are praying for us," Harmon said.

"I want you all to know that I pray for you every day. I love you. I thank God for the sacrifices you are willing to make for Him. You are always on my heart," Hiram said.

While he was in Swaziland, Dr. Reynolds and Rev. Schmelzenbach went to see the assistant commissioner for the British government.

"Sirs," Dr. Reynolds said, "our church, the Church of the Nazarene, is a new church. We have recently been allowed to open work in Swaziland. We thank you for letting us come to Swaziland to evangelize the people. We are interested in buying land in several places. We wish to build churches, schools, and a hospital."

The commissioner listened to Dr. Reynolds' request. Then he said, "Dr. Reynolds, we will be delighted to have you open schools and hospitals and homes for young girls. Wherever you can get consent from the local chiefs, you are welcome to build churches. I'll do my best to get you free grants of land for hospitals."

The missionaries were very excited. They had prayed for new land. Now they could have it.

While he was in Swaziland, Dr. Reynolds also ordained Harmon Schmelzenbach. Now Harmon was Rev. Schmelzenbach. Dr. Reynolds appointed Rev. Schmelzenbach as superintendent of the Africa Field of the Church of the Nazarene.

When Hiram felt his work in Swaziland was finished, he made plans to sail back to New York. He was eager to see Stella and his children. He had been gone for months. He planned to sail on a ship called the *Galatia*. The ship was delayed, so he found another one. While they were stopped in German West Africa, the captain received orders to change his course. Because of World War I, they were to go at once to a neutral port. The captain sailed for Brazil.

In Rio de Janeiro, Brazil, Hiram tried to buy a ticket on a ship called the *Indian Prince*. As he stood in line to buy his ticket, Hiram heard a Voice say, "Better not!" Hiram looked around to see who had spoken. No one was there.

Hiram Reynolds in Africa

Again he started to buy his ticket. Again the Voice said, "Better not!"

He looked around again. He saw no one.

Hiram held his money out to pay for his ticket. Again the Voice said, "Better not!"

This time he knew God was warning him not to sail on the *Indian Prince*. He couldn't understand what was happening. Hiram knew that he could trust God's voice.

Hiram bought a ticket on another ship, the *Oriana*. It was going the long way home. Hiram didn't understand why he couldn't take the *Indian Prince*. But, he obeyed God.

Three days later Hiram understood. He learned that the *Galatia* had been captured. He also learned that the *Indian Prince* had been sunk by an enemy warship. Everyone on the ship had been killed. God had spared Hiram's life again.

The *Oriana* made several stops before it reached New York. Hiram stayed a month in Scotland. While there, he talked with the leaders of other holiness churches. He talked to them about the Church of the Nazarene. However, it was 1915 before they agreed to merge with the Church of the Nazarene.

Finally, after 10 *l-o-n-g* months, Hiram arrived in New York. He stopped in Pittsburgh to visit a married daughter. Then he took a train to Kansas City and home!

"Hiram! I can't believe you're home!" Stella said, hugging her husband.

"It sure is wonderful to be home," Hiram said.

After a few days of rest, Dr. Reynolds and Dr. Bresee met to discuss the historic trip.

"Hiram," said Dr. Bresee, "I have read all your reports from your travels. It seems as though your first missionary trip was very successful."

"I think so too," Dr. Reynolds answered. "What impressed me most about our wonderful missionaries is all the sacrifices they are making to answer God's call for their lives. They never complain about the changes they have to make in their way of living. They are all happy serving the Lord."

Dr. Reynolds strongly urged the church to send more missionaries to Africa. Rev. Schmelzenbach needed more help.

The missionaries were not the only ones who did not complain. While Dr. Reynolds was on his tour, he slept on dirt floors and rode in rickshaws, springless carts, and covered wagons. He traveled under India's hot tropical sun and through Africa during the malaria season. No matter how unpleasant the conditions, Dr. Reynolds never complained.

Hiram Reynolds in Indian cart

He ate what the missionaries ate. He slept where the missionaries slept. He prayed with them, cried with them, and rejoiced with them.

6

Farewell, Stella!

After Dr. Reynolds had been home for several months, he decided to make another trip to the mission field. He hated to leave his family again so soon, but the work had to be done. While traveling, he wrote these words:

Dearest Stella,

The last few weeks have been very exciting. The Lord has helped me in many ways. I've helped the missions in Palestine get permission to have a church without having an orphanage. It's wonderful to see the Lord work in these countries.

I wish you were here with me. I miss you.

Love,
Hiram

Back home again, Dr. Reynolds had many duties as a general superintendent, but he continued to work for missions. He prayed for the missionaries every day. He wanted them to have enough food to eat, enough clothes to wear, and enough money to do God's work. He traveled to churches across the United States to raise money for the missionaries. There never seemed to be enough time to do everything that needed to be done.

In October 1919 Hiram and Stella were at the General Assembly in Kansas City. A special foreign missionary service was held on Thursday night. Dr. Reynolds was in charge. To add interest, he dressed in his oriental costume.

At the end of the service, pledges were taken for missionary work. At midnight it was announced that $1 million had been pledged, to be paid over the next four years. As everyone rejoiced, Dr. Reynolds offered to sell his oriental costume, piece by piece, and give the money to the missionary offering. Everyone had a good time as various individuals bought the costume—coat, slippers, helmet, walking stick, shield and spear, and a Japanese Bible. This money, plus later pledges, made a total of $1,004,075 for the offering.

Hiram was so happy he could hardly go to sleep that night. "Over a million dollars, Stella!" he said in wonder. "Just think what that will do on the mission fields."

The years passed by quickly. Dr. Reynolds worked hard to raise money to send to missionaries. They were always on his mind and heart.

In 1928 Hiram had a scary experience. "Mrs. Reynolds," the doctor said, "I have some bad news for you. Your husband has had a heart attack. He is resting right now. We won't know for two days whether or not he will make it."

"May I visit him now?" asked Mrs. Reynolds.

"Of course," the doctor said, "but only for a few minutes."

Stella quietly walked into Hiram's room. He looked so strange. He was usually a bundle of energy, but now he was quiet! Stella knelt beside the bed. "God, please heal my husband's heart. I need him so much," she prayed.

A few weeks passed. Dr. Reynolds got stronger and stronger. In a few days he could go home.

"Hiram," his doctor ordered, "you may go home on the following conditions:

"1. You will have to sit down when you preach.

"2. You will not be allowed to do a lot of walking.

"3. When you feel yourself getting tired—rest."

But Dr. Reynolds soon was working as hard as before.

"Hiram, you have to slow down," Stella urged. "If you don't, you're going to have another heart attack."

"I know, Stella," Hiram agreed. "But there's so much work to do!"

The people Dr. Reynolds worked with also felt he was working too hard.

"What can we do?" they asked. "We can't make him retire. He's one of the founders of our church."

"Why don't we create a new office for him?" someone suggested. "We could call it general superintendent emeritus! Then he can continue to serve the Church of the Nazarene for the rest of his life and not have to be elected. What do you think?"

The motion was passed. Dr. Reynolds became the first general superintendent emeritus in the Church of the Nazarene.

In 1934, at age 80, Dr. Reynolds had a second heart attack. "Stella," he said weakly, "I have no

Hiram and Stella Reynolds

choice now but to retire. My heart can't keep up with me!"

When he was allowed to go home, Hiram took very good care of himself—much to Stella's delight! He and Stella thought of a way they could continue to help the missionaries, without overworking. They made a giant prayer chart. They drew a map of the mission fields. Then they wrote the number

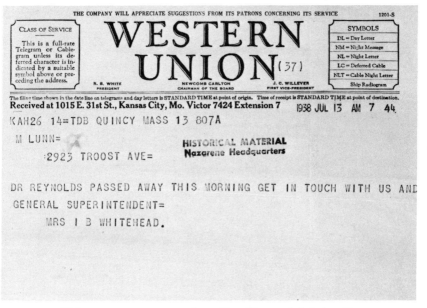

THE COMPANY WILL APPRECIATE SUGGESTIONS FROM ITS PATRONS CONCERNING ITS SERVICE   1201-S

CLASS OF SERVICE

This is a full-rate Telegram or Cablegram unless its deferred character is indicated by a suitable symbol above or preceding the address.

R. B. WHITE
PRESIDENT

WESTERN UNION (37)

NEWCOMB CARLTON
CHAIRMAN OF THE BOARD

J. C. WILLEVER
FIRST VICE-PRESIDENT

SYMBOLS

DL = Day Letter
NM = Night Message
NL = Night Letter
LC = Deferred Cable
NLT = Cable Night Letter
Ship Radiogram

The filing time shown in the date line on telegrams and day letters is STANDARD TIME at point of origin. Time of receipt is STANDARD TIME at point of destination.

Received at 1015 E. 31st St., Kansas City, Mo. Victor 7424 Extension 7   1938 JUL 13 AM 7 44

KAH26 14=TDB QUINCY MASS 13 807A

M LUNN=

2923 TROOST AVE=

HISTORICAL MATERIAL
Nazarene Headquarters

DR REYNOLDS PASSED AWAY THIS MORNING GET IN TOUCH WITH US AND GENERAL SUPERINTENDENT=

MRS I B WHITEHEAD.

Telegram announcing Dr. Reynolds' death

of people who lived on each mission field. They also wrote the name of each missionary next to the name of the country where he or she served.

Hiram and Stella got up to pray for missionaries at 6:00 each morning.

In March 1938 Dr. Reynolds became very ill. His doctor made him stay in bed for 17 weeks.

On July 13, 1938, just four days before his 59th wedding anniversary, Dr. Reynolds went to be with his Lord. He was 84 years old.

Dr. Reynolds had been a general superintendent for 25 years. He had also been responsible for the missionary work in the Church of the Nazarene from 1907 to 1932—25 years. He was truly "Mr. Foreign Missionary."

Bibliography

Hinshaw, Amy. *In Labors Abundant.* Kansas City: Nazarene Publishing House, n.d.

Lunn, M. *Mr. World Missionary.* Kansas City: Nazarene Publishing House, 1968.

Miller, Basil. *Out Under the Stars.* Kansas City: Nazarene Publishing House, 1941.

Young, Bill. *Boys Are What Men Are Made Of.* Kansas City: Nazarene Publishing House, 1975.